OUT O

By

Roy Wilkinson

Age
The old watch is cast into a drawer
to await being stumbled upon.

For Penny whose support
and encouragement have sustained me

Roy Edwin Wilkinson

Designed and produced by
George Mann Publications
Easton, Winchester,
Hampshire SO21 1ES
01962 779944

Text & illustrations copyright © Roy Wilkinson 2003

All rights reserved.
No part of this publication may
be reproduced, stored in a retrieval
system, or transmitted in any form or
by any means, electronic, mechanical,
photocopying, recording or otherwise,
without the prior permission
of the copyright holders

A CIP catalogue record for this book
is available from the British Library

ISBN 0-95-416349-4

George Mann Publications

The Poems

Can You Remember? 5

Beads 5

Heaven and Hell 6

Hark To 7

Dawn Woman 7

Night's Coming 8

Red Books of Knowledge 9

In a Bar Mirror 11

Dunvegan Bay 12

Entwined 13

Stinsford Church 13

Awakening 14

On the Beach 15

Blind Memory 15

Stargazer 16

Rock Remembered 17

Winter 17

Somnolent Days 18

Your Gifts	19
My Father	20
Not Mine!	25
Homecoming	26
Railway Arch	27
Not a Mark: 1943	28
Bill Tatters	29
Sharing	33
A Moment in Time	33
In the Dark	34
Room	35
Beasts?	36
Pointless Remorse	39
Between	40

Can You Remember?

Can you remember
When a letter
Made the heart leap
When the words sank
To the souls depth
Like water into sand?

Beads

I thread a string of days
with precious beads,
Pearls of pure delight
that never knew a shell.

Heaven and Hell

Why am I here with
Aching back, freezing feet,
Thoughts playing leap-frog
From sorrow to wit?
What place has a chuckle
Or even a tear at this
Hour of mans lowest ebb
When someone of sense
Would be in bed?
Why do I bleed so easily
From the prick of words
Of tiredness born?
Perhaps the truth is
Terribly simple –
Your smile is my heaven,
Your frown my hell!

Hark To

Hark to the beat of the tribal drum
Hark to the beat of the blazing sun
Hark to the beat of the reggae dancer
Hark to the beat of the ardent lover
Hark to the beat of the hearts trip-hammer
Hark to the sound of the negro singer
Hark to the measure of the pendulum clock
Hark to your feet as onward you go
Hark to the rhythm of things that grow!

Dawn Woman

All that's good of womans warmth
Is there at dawn awakening.
Her fragrance of earth and pine,
Her eyes still full of dreaming,
Unaware of easy grace,
Of the hearts catch at her smile,
Langorous, face wild hair framed,
Oh! the sweet fall of her breast!
Where words to speak my pleasure?
God, she says, I feel a mess!

Night's Coming

High hill brow beneath
Trees darkly club
In companionship,
Tawny walls bear
Gemstone eyes,
Gleaming.

Overhead, light paints
A masterwork.
Invisible birds
Converse; air cool
Wafts, flowery perfume.

A world exhaling
Soft breathy sighs,
Awaits the first star
To presage night's
Imminent coming.

Red Books of Knowledge

En-cyclo-paedia
Set of ten
Index (ignored, boring)
Leatherette
Red covers
Vol. One, ab-cab
In gold
Blue-edged pages
Photographs...
Wonders!

At four I knew
Where hid
Niagara falls
Salome dancing
Queen Mary...
Launched.

Electricity gen-er-ators
Hoover Dam
Blast furnaces
Tornado, twister
New York
Zulu warrior...
Naked.

Victoria and Albert...hall
Brer Rabbit
Camel train
Flying Scotsman
Handel, Turner
Fighting Temeraire...
Sunset.

King Canute
Puzzles...
Hampton Maze
Pyramids three
Seven wonders...
Lost.

Constellations
Zodiac
Tim-Buk-Too
Beethoven's scowl
Florence Nightingale
Berkley Square
Epsom Derby
Light Brigade...
Charging.

Professor Picard
Diving bell
Big Ben
Stonehenge
Beneath the sea
Dinosaurs
Dentistry
Radio waves...
Magic!

Too soon
Red to pink
Blue to grey
Schoolboy become
Innocent wonder...
Gone.

In a Bar Mirror

The raw intensity in her eyes shocked,
A Hoover Dam of grief straining
Against determination not to yield,
A fierce will to hold on, to subdue
The horrors rising from an inner pit.
Eyes as stark as a lightning flash
Mirrored reflected humiliation.

Shaken, I turned away.

A blue-uniformed man surrounded her
Radiating anger, hands clutching,
"C'mon, I've paid for bloody dinner"
white-faced, the woman slipped his bull-rush.
Her whispered "Shall we go" in ice.
Uniform, red-faced, blundered after her.
"Bitch" he spat, emptying into the street.

Dunvegan Bay

Far out all diamantine sparkle
Water races to meet plunging sun.
Islets, scattered beads, change
Gold to fire, to purple.
No bird wings overhead
No creature crawls below,
No footstep crunches sand,
Hush, only broken by
The suck and gurgle of
Shallow receding pools.
Creeping gaunt-rock shadows
Spear the bay,
This the worlds end
In awesome quiet
Dying with the day.

Entwined

When I see beauty
I think of you.
With every breath
I speak your name.
With every pulse
Love for you flows,
All strands of thought
Entwined by you.
No longer may I know
Where I end
And you begin.

Stinsford Church

Stained glass filters
Choral notes of
Splintered light,
Sanctified air imbues
Ecclesiastical odours,
Organ vibrations
Sombre shadows haunt.
A tiny window lights,
With exquisite blues and golds,
A small recess : here the heart!
Surely generations have stood
Inspired to contemplation,
The least shedding
A greater light –
As may the pauper's mound
Be more eloquent
Of man's estate,
Than a marble tomb.

Awakening

With infinite patience
Dawn softly respires
Gently seeping colour
Across cool hush,
A creaking gate allows
The leak of footsteps.
A restive child somewhere
Kissed to quietude,
The brightening chorus
Of newday stretches
Over the dreaming land
Born on wings of light,
A waking sigh of love.

The nasal bicker of
A motor cycle
Shatters the quiet to
Nerve-edged fragments,
The modern Kraken wakes
Rumbles through the lanes,
Gleaming beetles driven
By worker ants,
Clot in veinous roadways,
Throb to new-age drums,
Everywhere frantic rush
By the clock ruled,
Dawns peace un-noticed, died.

On the Beach

Love's blanket wrapped
Us close around
Dispelling doubt.
Confirming that first
Long enraptured look
With sunshine bursts
Of smiles.

Blind Memory

Eyes of memory
Are blind to truth
Forgetfulness inbred
Dusty excuses lie
Thickly over fabric
Mind dare not pick
Fearing a painful
Unravelling.

Stargazer

Remote, you winked at me
While searchlights wandered
And I, short-trousered stood
Amazed.

A cold December night I
Rode beneath your gaze
And saw your pale dying
At dawn.

Black velvet Cyprus night
Sten-gun in my hand
And I the Plough followed
For sign.

In Spanish hills by night
Deep dark pools you cast,
And I stumbled onward,
Still lost.

Remote, you winked at me
Behind the full moon,
And I howled at you:
I love!

And this you cannot do
For all that you mock.
And I, though soon to pass,
Still gaze!

Rock Remembered

Have you ever
Walked rocky roads
Seen a stone, one
Among many,
Yet remembered?

Was it the shape,
Position, perhaps,
Self-possession
Lent it meaning?

Face in the crowd?
Yes? Is that what
Haunted me, its
Insignificance?

My own reflected?

Winter

The mallows are dead,
They will not grow again –
Their profusion of joy
A fading memory.
A ghost of myself
Amid the shambles
I long for Spring.

Somnolent Days

Somnolent radiant summer hours
Languidly stretching, easy golden
Warmth, drooping eyes protectively
Against dancing glare, from leaf and stone.
Timeless moments, softly murmured words
Sweet smell of grass insect-drone busy,
Sunward faintly smiling faces turned,
Patterns of shadows on lolling limbs.
A canted coffee mug, fly on rim,
Flowers shimmering, bleaching wood,
Beyond the hedge, tarmac, flashing cars,
Fume hurry outside, peace here within.

Your Gifts

You taught me how to smile,
Open a 2CV window.
You taught me how to love
And not squash garden slugs.
You taught me to live with my faults
And get on with the washing-up.
You taught me true values
And to live with odd socks.

You gave me happiness
And took my selfish ways.
You gave me a loving home
And took me to your heart.
You gave me a taste of heaven
And ate most of the ice-cream.
You gave me precious time,
And delighted in shocking me.

My Father

Norman, shorter than me.
On his face a fixed
Expression of distrust
As if life and all men
Either were cheating him
Now, or surely would tomorrow.

Favourite words –
Bah! And Humph!
Visitors-few,
Barely tolerated.
One look-conversation
Killed!

Born in a Walsall
Back to back,
One of seven
Bare-footed and
Bare-arsed
Told how, as a child, how he
Would fetch shopping for
A woman down the road.
Of the promised penny
Or orange that never
Materialised.

That of all things this small
Betrayal he chose to relate,
Showed how it had coloured
His attitude
All of his life.

Education poor,
Terminated early,
Painfully learned
Power corrupts –
Canings, less for sins
Than teacher frustration.

A good mind, but
Not the tools to
Make best use of it.
Paid for home tuition
Postal courses –
English, maths,
How to think correctly.

Entered the new R.A.F.
Three years in Arabia
Gulf of Aden,
Radio operator,
Sun-scorched wastes.
Invalided out
Skin disease:
Red-raw patches.

Blighty 1934
Unemployment
Passed Civil service
Entrance exams
Became an airport radio controller
At which level
he stayed.

Norman was never
A social being
Always the odd-man-out,
Who would not,
Suffer fools gladly.

How such a solitary
Socially graceless man
Won my mother-
Lilian, Alderman's daughter,
College matriculated
Gregarious party-goer –
Always a mystery!
Yet Norman lured her
Away from David
Of the red M.G.

Newly married
They settled for
A bare rented cottage
In tiny Harleston.
For Lilian, when I arrived,
the party days were over.

He was often away.
Isle of Lewis, Harris,
Stornaway,
Sent boxes of kippers.
When home, sanctuary:
His radio room,
Never to be violated
By a curious child.

Of me he would say
(if pressed)
'Wants his brains testing.'

I hugged him twice.

The first time when
My mother died.
He sat in his chair
Crying, staring at
her tagged bag
of personal effects.

The second time
at the Cottage Hospital
Norman taken in
Suffering heart pain
nose bloody –
an earlier fall –
aplogetic doctor,
These things happen."

"How are you, Dad?"
Oxygen mask
removed
"Bah! They've run out of blood,
had to send for it!"
(contempt for their lack).

"Two days more in
this damned bed,"
Rush of love!
I held him
He felt shrunken.

"Humph!
What about Spain?"
"Oh! Going soon –
"NO! NO! the mortgage?"
"Sorry, it's all..."
"Get me the bottle!"
Urgent gesture below
I bent, found it,
Straightened.

He was gone.
To the last himself.

Side ward.
Hand still warm.
Frown forever fixed
as if distrusting death.

"You're OK now, Dad
sleep well."

Why?
Did I whisper?

Not Mine!

It is not mine, this face
With haunted eyes,
This weary stranger in
The glass. Not me!
Whose parody of a
Smile? It's not mine
This wrinkled puppet-head,
It is NOT mine!
Not mine, I say, NOT MINE!
Yet...
    I dab the toothpaste
Dribbles from its chin
Brush greying hair
And wherever I go,
Take IT with me!

Homecoming

Dogs ears spring alert –
Two noses pointing
There! Tyres on grit
The crunch of handbrake
Clunk of car door.
Dogs all ready at the stair
I hear the gate creak
Your weary footsteps coming up,
Three sets soul-windows
Expectantly await...
Your key turning –
My heart unlocks
Leaping like our dogs
As inward you come,
Bringing light in a smile.
Home a deeper meaning takes,
Its essential heart restored.

Railway Arch

Beside the Stour
A truncated arch of brick
To nowhere leads,
Rising up from winter mists,
Roiling reminder of
Boiler-fired breath,
Railway days of
Billowing smutty swathes –
Of jetting clanking engines,
Setting iron rails to groan
And sheep to huddled flight.
Is that sulphorous smoke
Or rotting leaves I smell?
Half-closed eyes…dead weeds
And weary grasses fade.
See…sleepers, twin gleaming rails
In distant illusion met.
Listen!
Is that a gull…or the mournful
Whistle of a long-past train?

Not a Mark: 1943

Louder than all the others-much louder
Aimed at me! Whistle piercing,
My scream searing upward
Sheared by a deafening roar
Quivering silence…
I struggled from under Mum
Dust sifting into the shelter
Beneath the dining table
We huddled shaking.
Suspended until the "All clear".

Next day, next street
    I found the impact site:
A house half eviscerated
Exposed a roomless upstairs fireplace
Transfers fixed to the tile surround
Pluto, Donald Duck, Mickey Mouse.
"Not a mark on them!"
I heard a neighbour say"All four of them, still sitting there".
Incongruously, a table and chairs
Stood amid smoking rubble in the street.

Half a century later, memory haunts
Coloured Disney transfers still clear and bright.
Pluto, Donald Duck, Mickey Mouse.

Bill Tatters

At eight I was a white strip
With knobs for knees, recovering
From being an evacuee,
From scabies, impetigo, malnutrition
And (undiagnosed) T.B.

At the end of war, my parents
Moved to decimated Coventry,
From the Cheylesmore Estate.
I was sent to Green Lane school.
Bill Tatters was there!

Bill came from a poor area
Where street fights were common,
(Already he was scarred)
fists Bill understood,
words are for Fairies!

Looking back, I can see
That forty children had
The nous to become Bill's
Followers, egging him on.
Only one did not. Me.

A withdrawn only child,
Unaggressively, quietly spoken,
I had no interest in Bill,
His passion for football
Or the daily kick-abouts.

His dislike for me – instant!
My time of terror became
Morning playtime, when
He and his followers would
Descend on me with glee.

I bore the beatings stoically
Without fighting back – was there
Something wrong with me?
Was I to blame that
No-one liked me?

I spoke to my Dad
"Hit him back, son, hard!"
He showed me a throw
And an upper-cut.
I was appalled.

Hit Bill Tatters! No!
Maiming would follow
He would just kill me –
Cheered on by his mates.
Better to endure the bullying.

Instead, I learned every route,
Every hole in hedge
Hidden gate or gap
As a means to come and go
Avoiding Bill T.

Still he found me –
The waking nightmare
Haunted my dreams,
Bedwetting adding to my misery.

Hate Bill I did not,
oddly, in truth,
I quite admired him;
How good to be strong
Utterly fearless.

Nineteen-forty-six.
A bitter winter,
I, shaking with cold,
Saw Bill and the pack
Closing in on me.

Why then? Why that day
Did something inside me
Break out in total
Explosive anger?
Devastating me?

I braced myself
For the jeers, the blows,
Usually to my stomach.
Then, as Bill swung his fist,
My knee drove upward.

I was horrified, amazed
To see Him lying
Face down on the ground
Groaning and snuffling,
His followers aghast.

They began to howl:
"Do him, Bill! Kill Him!"
Bill leapt up snarling,
head down he charged.
I hit him again.

An uppercut with
All my slender rage,
Bill fell down bleeding
His nose mis-shapen.
The mob circled outraged.

Bill was escorted
Inside by the class,
While I stood outside
Shivering in the cold,
Sick with violence.

Brought before the head,
I was labelled a bully.
My parents were informed
My mother disgusted.
My Dad gave me a wink!

Of course Bill came back.
A jab on the arm
In passing, both knowing
It was for pride's sake,
Not worth anger now.

Sharing

My eyes weep not your tears
My pain rives not your nerves
Inside I cry, kiss your eyes,
Is helpless watching less a hurt?
No wafer our communion
Needs, lest it be a cigarette.
Our blood not wine sanctified
But tears in a whisky glass.
The quiet of our church is
Broken by a throaty laugh.
Could be no other way but this.

A Moment in Time

La Pacheca – a pile of white boxes
Clustered against a Spanish hill,
black breakers, balconies, pantile rooves
Baking in the sun, which,
Hot golden white, sears the eye,
Lances through shutters, patterning tiles.
My love and I curl together naked
On a cool cream bed. "O Mio Bambino Caro" plays softly
In the next room.
Emotional feelings of immense comfort, peace,
                            swell hugely within us.
Nothing is said. Our gentle embrace
Tells all, as a single tear gilds my wife's lashes,
Before slowly
Seeping away.

In the Dark

I sometimes get the feeling
Theres something in the dark,
Something close behind me
That stalks me in the park.

I often look behind me
(in a casual way)
how loud my footsteps are.
Worried? course not, I'd say.

When at last I reach my door
Fumbling for my Yale key,
Too loud my harsh breathing
To hear what followed me.

Sometimes at night I'll wake
Who's there? I'll want to call
Keep still-although I know
Theres nothing there at all.

Remember then my childhood
The Bogeyman would come
To punish me for sin
Be sent for by my Mum.

My dressing-gown on its peg
In gloom become his form
Its MEEE! his awful voice
Wails in the thrashing storm.

Now that I am older, Mum,
You having long since died,
I wish you had known my fears.
Too often then I cried.

Room

Room, silence swollen
Odour of flowers
Polish, mothballs
Fabric, dust dried
Drawn against the light.

Echoes, laughter past
Whispers, wailing.
Ice-cold white death
Hurls embalmed need
For a deeper place
Against confining walls.

Beasts?

Once, man and beast together lived
On the land where they were born,
A mutual dependence.
You called it Husbandry.
You did not abuse us
Strip us of our dignity
Make a horror of our lives.

Now mankind lives in cities
Unknowing of our needs.
Old ties and bonds are gone.
What can you feel when all you know
Are anonymous dyed pieces
Prepackaged on a shelf?

On your walls you hang pictures
Of peaceful country scenes,
Fat sows and piglets rooting
In the sunlit open fields –
Not packed in concrete pens
Consuming their own kind.

Nursery walls you cover
With cartoons of beasts and birds.
"Look, Darling, that's a moo-cow.
It gives us lovely milk"
Who hears us in the night –
Pitifully calling when
Too soon our calves are gone?

"Here's a chicken, baby dear,
it lays your breakfast egg"
Do you tell of wire boxes
thousands to a shed, of
clipped beaks, useless legs?

The farmer is shown smiling
Always prosperous, well fed,
Not forced by economics
To put a shotgun to his head.
Hail god the supermarket!
Hail god the almighty buck!

Now that we are sick
Your slaughtermen have come.
Theres no mercy in their hearts –
Not even for their own –
Obscene our bloating carcasses
Piled high like Belsen Jews.
We, in numbing numbers,
Just lost balance of trade.

At Easter will you buy a card
Showing gambolling spring lambs?
Will you, that soon, forget
Piles of blazing corpses like
A scene from Dante's Hell?

Deadly dancers, we leave
Silent fields a testament
To the consequence of greed.
Be thankful you see the sky,
You will not be force-fed,
Overdosed on hormones,
In your food find human flesh.

You don't have to become vegans :
All life lives by others death,
But be wise, merciful gods,
Do not rob us of everything
That makes lowly lives worthwhile,
Lest you pile up under heaven
Man's own dread funeral pyre!

Pointless Remorse

Past is a land where none may dwell
Its lessons are learned
My life is now, I say
The future a page to be turned.

Yet, fragments of memory
Slivers glass-sharp
Prick my spirit feet.
How fortunate I am!
Most memories are sweet.

Still, when I recall how
I was less a man
Than I might have been
I writhe in pointless remorse
My face, behind a smile,
Unseen.

Between

I am between sleeping and waking
Between truth and lie
Between staying and leaving.
I divide sanity from madness
I split reality from dream
A river of thought between flesh and spirit.
I am between breathing and sighing
Between decision and consequence,
I am twilight between light and dark.